The Nagasaki Elder

Anna

Antony Owen

House of Lords 6/12/22

Best

V.

Published in the United Kingdom in 2017
by V. Press,
10 Vernon Grove,
Droitwich,
Worcestershire,
WR9 9LQ.

ISBN: 978-0-9935508-2-9

Printed in the U.K. by Imprint Digital, Seychelles Farm, Upton Pyne, Exeter EX5 5HY, on recycled paper stock.

V.

Contents

PART 1 – INFERNO

PART 2 – THE HUMAN BLITZ

For all survivors (Hibakusha)

"Suffering is a treasure, so that I can share my stories with you."

(Hibakusha)

INFERNO

The queen of new Hiroshima

After Akira Kurosawa

On a playground where children vanished into black magic,
she played chess without the pieces, showing me
how old age twists bones like steel climbing frames
where fingerprints remain on rails, heaven denied.

She taught me to understand Hiroshima,
we must first lose our pawns
and see ourselves as Gods
in charge of games.

Only when the board is barren, we see empires
are realms of pot-bellied maggots in human thrones
stacked thirty foot high.

She told me this playground was her fourth layer of skin
and, if I looked closely through her continents of scars,
I would see artifacts of a child in a permanent frock:
the princess of old Hiroshima crowned by laurel flames.

Pearl Harbour

After Jacques Gaucheron

In Hiroshima, there are many pearl harbours
burning in waters of survivors' eyes and I
have watched these oysters prised open through grief –
a pale glaucoma where the photographed dot
explodes *that day* in the grief-linished pupils.

In Hiroshima, there were many boats on fire,
floating in the six rivers like Viking burials,
thousands of rags anchored to the old place
from limbs caught on trees' rigor mortis –
did they never want to leave this city of water and fire?

In Hiroshima, they harvest pearls in the inland sea
and some use these spent shells for soup bowls
or ashtrays, but some hold the tale to their ears
and hear the dead whispering to those who drank them:
"I am a shadow that once cast a boy, hiding in the open."

Senryu (I)

Little boy humming,
dragonfly strumming, gamma
numbing, black rain coming.

The last fare collector of Hiroshima

They found her fingers in a jelly of yen,
her skin one with the standard issue fare-bag –
a dove in a sen of silver to go to the mountains,
oh, if only she went.

I have read of a woman
who cooled her burns with figs and persimmon.
She pared away old skin for years; it was the finest paper,
writing its kanji into the papyrus sky. I wish I knew her.

In the ritual of tea-making,
I learnt how to sip from a widow's eyes
and learn that some stories are like Hiroshima streetcars –
they always arrive on time then the hour takes them.

They found her omen in the evening crow
hopping by the river: it is time to see how atoms rise
when another survivor dies;
their story closes with their eyelids.

I have read of a God-fearing woman
who feared man so much more;
she sliced a cucumber each night for years to cool her skin
and hate had left her years ago with five generations of
fishermen
        horse-breakers
                librarians
                        mothers
                                fathers
                                        fare-collector.

Sen: Old Japanese coins. The sen was taken out of currency in 1953.

Homes of wood and paper

For Sueko

Look at how survivors live now,
hidden away in honeycombed tenements,
each throbbing from their terrible hives.

Look at their contact with the outside world,
satellite dishes face skyward with tongues out
just like those rivers of floating souls.

Look at the washing lines starved of clothes –
limbs of white chiffon dancing on the dead wind
in crumpled stripes of star-spangled banners –

the emperor's new clothes?

Once they lived in homes of wood and paper,
with mothers who knew their myrrh of birth,
survivors today are twice-born miracles.

In homes of wood and paper, mountains appeared,
sky ran red like seppuku, sun was disembowelled
and black holes of mouths were pails of bleak rain.

Look at the lampposts, twisted black as liquorice,
bow-legged structures singing ballads of melted iron;
explain to me where homes of wood and paper go?

Explain to me in *simplified Japanese.*

Torch

For Keiko

Little boy made a flower,
ploughed a city with fire,
watered in black rain.

Little girl made a wish and fishtails,
reflecting in the koi-red bayou –
all they found were hair pins.

Little flies hummed godless sermons –
from pulpits of bone, the spires soar;
look, Hiroshima is our torch.

Little silver eagles drop vengeful eggs.
A phoenix does not rise from ashes –
only a *procession of ghosts.*

Green tomato

Look at those boats of bone in rivers –
last night their eyes were lighthouses
shining blue and brown in natural darkness.

Look at that shape ripped apart like rags –
the pinafore spoke what sex it was;
she died with a green tomato punctured on red lips.

Look at that crucifix smelted to *its* skin;
her lifeline blew in the Fahrenheit wind –
three children, living long and healthy.

Look at all these unripe tomatoes in mouths –
they died the moment they sucked the juice,
made another mountain on school playgrounds.

Black rain

For Yumiko

You were the sun
that stole a rainbow
from arcs of Hiroshima bridges,
and how you chose your colours.
First, magnesium reds twined like blood in water,
then you stole blue and brown from eyes of children,
but black is what you wanted the most, a certain shade.

So, you mixed the colours
with burning hair and wind,
unshackled the shadows free from all their flesh,
but they wept in the blood-drenched dusk
and the only way to return to Hiroshima
was to weep as black rain to where they had risen,
nourishing the scorched tundra in eggshell raindrops
until they exploded as oleanders.

Purple chalk

Years after the bomb startled water,
koi engulfed the egg-flecked banks,
spawning shockwaves of life.

Years after the ill star was born,
shy women revealed themselves
to men who took their blood and husbands.

Months after the first silent births,
a mother took her unnamed life
and then her soul in a whispering rill.

Weeks after, this girl with the handprint face
explained she was counting to ten, then a flash
printed hide and seek on her face.

Days after, a boy wrote his name in purple chalk –
his yo-yoing eyes spilled across his frame;
they washed his feet before he died.

Before he died, he asked why me?
The boy on the human bonfire
gulped, koi-mouthed, at the sky.

To feed a Nagasaki starling

She said don't go to the shadows without water –
I have tried to erase him for sixty-four years
and my wrists are tired;
I have scrubbed the darkness of my son
so he could be buried at last in sunlight.

Don't go to my son without removing your shoes –
I have tried to bathe him with prayers and carbolic
but he only gets blacker;
I have lived for ninety-nine years
and starlings are beginning to land by my feet.

Don't wind the paralysed clock,
it is rebuilding the world with seared hands –
I have tried to turn back time
but God will not allow it in Nagasaki;
I had tried to make another child but gave birth to pink curd.

Don't tell them my name,
and look me in the face when you see him –
I have tried to understand
why ink is only spilled by vaporised kin;
I have tried to write a haiku
for the willow which strokes my son.

Don't disturb my son
when the raven plays in the shape of his spectre –
I have tried to shoo it away and it quarrels with my broomstick;
I have tried to tell my son that he was ten yards from living.

I have tried to feed a Nagasaki starling
when it drank the black rain;

I have tried to get it to sing so this wraith could be comforted –
don’t disturb my grave and desecrate me
with twitching shadows.

The art of war (I)

For Fergus

The old Hiroshima trees in autumn scratch the ill wind till it bleeds in time for spring when the dead each blow a petal and their fragrant inferno engulfs a man coughing blossoms of blood from weak boughs of bone, but he is a strong root. He told me when spring leaves Hiroshima, all that remains of trees are fingers of the dead, holding birds that swept across sky like ashes, throwing their urn of shrieks to a scarlet sun hurling the war of blood inside. Every year, the cherry blossoms get redder and a zephyr sighs as they fall. The rivers in every petal are souls who drank the wrong rain; they are louder each year for the shadows that are lighter, spilled like quill pots of unwritten lives. Hiroshima streets are a *Pollock* canvas. From shockwaves of pure monsoon rain, the drip-drop dragonflies brush watercolours on grave-grey rivers and dusk-fall is an easel, yet the saddest artist twice drew a black orchid on a blue face.

Pollock refers to the works of artist Jackson Pollock.

Sketching of an atomic horse

"Why did the ants crawl back into the house just before the atom bomb was dropped?"
"Did they know of what was to come?"
A Coventry school student upon seeing 'Barefoot Gen'

In pastures of blank white pages,
someone captured a nag through graphite,
rubbing its lead mane in the dropped stars' corona.

Pencil on page is a cruel stable:
a nag lapping troughs of her wounds,
the hurled tongue green from ghosts of grass.

There is no shame in falling twice –
a neigh of hot hail stampedes the thoroughbred;
art pulls the drowned foal from eyes.

Honkawa School

For Hideko Okamoto

After sky-scraping flames,
a fire tsunami left you stranded –
open-mouthed like clams whispering of tragic shells.

When I set foot in your heart,
my steps were beating for all the dead school children,
cremated where they pat-a-caked.

At eight fifteen, a little boy bludgeoned the deafening gong,
and flesh soft as Japanese vowels
scarred the face of feverish earth.

Today the children made a sandstorm from their playground;
a boy kicked a ball, missing the goal,
yet he made me feel like celebrating.

The Nagasaki elder

Her first son was silent
as if refusing to weep from that beautiful slum –
the still yellow flower of Nagasaki took nine months to bloom.

Her first kiss was black rain
writing tragic symphonies on song-sheet glass;
her father is the boogeyman haunted by his own slivered face.

Her first period was jelly.
The shift mothers came trained to hold survivors,
do not say a word to the handsome doctor who writes for your
blood.

Her first revolution was spinning a potter's wheel anti-
clockwise;
re-shaping her family with Nagasaki clay, she said –
this is how water should feel.

Senryu (II)

In Nagasaki
sons kissed mothers through lint
writhing like silkworms.

Kamikaze song

"Nearby birds burst into flames in mid-air"
U.S. Department of Energy

I wonder what became of Nagasaki sparrows.
Story has it one flew headfirst into a little boat –
this was no inconvenience but they were startled.

I wonder how far they flew blinded for,
bellies filled with insects and dawn song –
earth-curve eyes pulled back to moonstone.

I hope they died on Japan's blotched face,
pressed freckles from blue corrupted eggs,
hatching man's miscarriage in the bloody new dusk.

Trolls of the Aioi Bridge

"Well come along! I've got two spears and I'll poke your eyeballs out at your ears; I've got besides two curling-stones, and I'll crush you to bits, body and bones."
From Three Billy Goats Gruff

Once upon a time in Hiroshima,
mothers read fairy tales and omens
of trolls under bridges to fearless children.

Atomic rivers were cauldrons of men,
women and children gobbled up into trolls.
Human monsters queued to join them.

I want to write a war poem without monsters
where all of us live happily ever after.

Senryu (III)

In Hiroshima
she folded into papier-
mâché origami

The ferryman

I often think of that unnamed road in Nagasaki
where the 'o' of her breast remained untouched by fire
as her daughter suckled to live through *Fat Man's* crucible.

I often think of the man who found them as Pompeii ornaments,
standing there knowing he would soon pay Charon at the shore,
as he drifted away from *Sake* and swords born of fire and water.

I often think of Nagasaki Mothers as sheets for their babies.
We are going to sleep in a manger of weird flames,
death will display us like screaming white logs.

I often think of those things the bomb breathed upwards –
tatami mats and door knobs found high in mountains,
dentures welded to the bones of a charred umbrella.

I choose to forget the image that made Charon weep –
East of the river *Ota,* when he suckled at the banks,
he saw a manger of skulls weeping crayfish.

Fat Man was the name of the atomic bomb dropped on Nagasaki. Several sources including The Washington Post, BBC and Atomic Bomb Museum refer to Fat Man as a nickname for Winston Churchill. Similarly, Little Boy, dropped on Hiroshima, refers to former American President Roosevelt who died in WW2 shortly before President Truman replaced him.

That woman in the ANA hotel

For Sadako Sasaki

Awaking in unforgettable fire,
that woman dressed in diamonds
would have worn glass all over her flesh.
That woman would not be proud of those rubies
spattering old flags of Nippon.
That woman would not be drinking *Evian*,
face down in the river of souls
black as niblets of ruined corn
nobody wants to harvest.

Spring letters

"Who will want children with me now?"
Hibakusha

Those trees write essays of blossom and fall,
and sometimes strike twigs of lightening
to show us that roots lie in all things,
branches bellow in our blood
of strange white lilies,
clockwork leukaemia
hands stop moving,
radioactive graves
jigsaw pictures of
petri dish ghosts.
Scalp Hiroshima –
we were human,
remember,
our roots
entwine;
inside we are all the same –
blossoms of blood capillaries.

How to make a Japanese flag

For Jose

Oh, skull of the new dropped sun,
I saw my bones in your photograph,
and the day I met my mother's face.

I am looking for our house with my hands,
these eyes are bluish milk in my fists;
I plucked them from my chest like a lotus.

There is a hunchback made of Hiroshima
against the sky; its head is flattening,
weeping darkness that little boys weep.

There are monsters writhing in lettuce.
It is cool here among the wet plants;
they are digging themselves to earthly death.

I am watching a young man fishing for
his mother – who used to make temples of clay
and wore a hat to keep away God's sun –

where eels would move in rivers like medusa hair,
fat from flesh of the split-second star.
The young man combs through bodies for weeks.

If you come here, don't tell the shadows they were flesh.
Do not touch hand-marks left on bridge rails –
they are lifelines painting the un-blossomed souls.

Oh, skull of the new dropped sun,
show me how to make a Japanese flag,
and I shall blow at the cloth of concrete sky.

The stars that wandered Hiroshima

"President Truman said he dropped the atomic bomb against those who had attacked Pearl Harbour and against those who were cruel to American Prisoners of war yet I was just a child like thousands of others whose life was ruined by war."
Survivor (Anon)

After wet shadows wept themselves pure,
she remembered the afterbirth of that new world,
galaxies of glimmering glass that roamed Hiroshima roads,
their last words of *"water"* honoured through survivors' eyes.

I have listened to the morbid anthems of cockroach and fly;
winners of war lay terrible jewels in human treasures.
Respect the dead and burn those foothills of flesh,
she said; she often awakes saying their names.

I have held the hand of an old Hibakusha –
it felt like the chest of a fallen gosling
in a city that felt like a cage
where people stared
at the telling scarf
worn in August
covering scars
she opened
just for me
to share
with
you,
us.

Nisei

"Having found the bomb, we have used it. We have used it in order to shorten the agony of war, in order to save the lives of thousands and thousands of young Americans."
President Truman, August 1945

Half Japanese and half American is labelled Nisei.
Half Irish and half American is labelled American.
All are capable of love and burning.
A blood orange is still an orange, and peels –
the flesh comes away in the hand so easily.
Three thousand Nisei died full deaths in Hiroshima,
more than nine eleven, more than seven seven.

Three thousand humans had half empty lives;
corpses stacked like wigwams on the pyre,
erased like jumpers by a dropped dividing star,
these new *states of death* saved American lives.
The blood of three thousand Nisei was a seventh river
flowing through Hiroshima into a half moon.

We build our nations from scripted words –
"We have used it against those who have starved
and beaten and executed American prisoners of war..."
– yet no child did this in the over-bombed cities.
These speeches of men playing Gods who unmake
are written from the ink of human darkness.

In the late 1970s America finally acknowledged the deaths of twelve American Prisoners of War who were killed by the Atomic bombing of Hiroshima.
Sources: The Nation, Boston Magazine(.com)

When children see fairy tales die

"A second kiss for Hirohito"
(Message written on the plutonium bomb nicknamed "Fat Man" which was dropped above Nagasaki.)

She said the autumn wind is just;
a scaffold of oak builds new seasons
so traipse upon its grave a meaningful walk
and breathe ghosts of your babes in white sheets of air.

She said the autumn trees are us;
they bend close to breaking yet sustain,
and banshees blow their short-lived blooms to remind us
roots are where we started and where our last day leads to.

I said the autumn dusk is our babe,
temporary reds bleed against the stillness,
yet daylight will return in rags that rinse from clouds
like old skin of permanent children who saw fairy tales die.

Senryu (IV)

Half-peeled mandarin:
warm torn skin, dimpled, fragrant
cloud vapours consumed.

Fat Man

"The statesman who yields to war fever must realise that once the signal is given, he is no longer the master of policy but the slave of unforeseeable and uncontrollable events."
Winston Churchill

Oh, ribbon weaver,
what did you weave in the war room
for Coventry?

Fine sky-blue yarns,
fat Havana halos, the prophetic ligature
for stained black saints.

Oh, war shepherd,
the mauling wolves embed our moon,
torn against our spire.

Toe tags queue for names –
a child they thought was a beam
was younger than your brandy.

Oh, ribbon weaver,
what will you weave for Dresden
from Coventry's stone elbows?

The Nagasaki bastard
they named after you
whistled like a soldier,

bloomed for the lotus flower,
your carbonised legacy.
Fat Man, fire, criminal.

Senryu (V)

Fat Man awakens,
devouring breath, birdsong sky.
Skeleton city.

Dragon girl

For the 20,000+ Korean women, men and children who perished in the atomic bombings of Hiroshima and Nagasaki.

In the atlas of uncertified madness,
she walked naked to the Y-shaped river,
smoke rolling from a red scaly mouth;
her silent yell split the peaceful atoms –
and this was winter nineteen forty-five,
when dragon girl dreaded the hatchling.

Someone told me these six rivers belch
for all the bodies force-fed in August.
Before dragon girl, there was Nabi,
who planted milk teeth and dreamt on them.
She awoke between a lintel on rooftops.

If you want to see Hiroshima, stay with me.
Have you ever seen a person truly reborn?
Dragon girl walked to the bridge and froze.
Named herself dragon girl, dragon girl.
All she said until winter of forty- five,
when her perfect daughter was born screaming –
Nabi yelled back, dragon girl, dragon girl,
to the miracle in swaddling dragon girl. Dragon girl.

The fisherman's daughter

After James Kirkup

Some things drag us back sad and heavy
like gipsy wagons concealing a cargo
of painted-over myths that peel us to grain.

Some things wake us in our temporary deaths –
a grey crop of hair my lover's lips flower through,
kissing closed eyes, her pencil-case prince.

Some things break open like Hiroshima clouds –
daffodil bulbs glowing out from trespassed darkness;
this is me, my love, head bowing to so much death.

Some things translate us from the font of human bone
carried by a fisher – his daughter's dress with a ghost
of her handprint flashed against the flora.

Some things never change, like those who dare not look,
who make their nuclear families in brittle little hamlets,
and teach their children never to play with matches.

The clown of Nagasaki circus

For John Hartley

She said that Nagasaki morgues
were babies born like blown-out candles.
Except for him, his birth skin smoking
from a stratosphere of uterus.

As a boy, she told him to love his face
when children yelled 'Tempura'.
He rolled the moon like a rice ball
and gave it to them.

As a young man, he was reborn in a circus lion's eye,
heavy and caged, yet in the monsoon savannah of those eyes
he was free.

She said his face was a map of old Nagasaki
and his lifelines were rivers where their father sailed
with lanterns of koi and mackerel.

As the Nagasaki clown, he learnt to be laughed at differently,
that children born perfect would love the dancing lion.

As the clown, he left the face they accepted in cotton balls;
the face they loved had the eyes of his mother.

Letter from the sun to man

"How can God-fearing men drop a bomb over a cathedral?"
A Coventry Evacuee

Dear human, I am dying slowly yet you murdered my sibling wind. You took her last breath on August sixth and ninth, *your sun* blew it back so fast it made my children vapour and shadow. Some of them made lakes in the sky, estuaries of red mixing with ebony rain – like cardinal cloaks spilling rosary beads, yet this was not the blood of God, this was yours.

Dear human, I am dying slowly, like that girl and that boy, and that boy and that girl, and to save ten thousand pages – for there are no trees left – let me say there is nothing here but death. Look at my daughter moon, her face looks sicker – she has seen a doll made of flesh, kokeshi white and limbless like moon. *Oh, what have you done, dear human?*

Dear human, this new flag of Japan shows my face – I am limbless of rays like my daughter moon. Our empires are now just islands of Hibakusha conquered in their wars of altered blood. My orphan nephews shall be peaceful now, please listen to the silence of Nagasaki streets and the noise of Nagasaki streets will disturb you like typhoons of Hiroshima butterflies.

Dear human, I am dying slowly,
yet I shall outlive you with your Mother
Earth.

Kokeshi dolls are considered a lucky charm to protect a home against fire. They are often limbless and made by craftsman in various prefectures across Japan.

Hell

After illustrations by survivors as featured in The Unforgettable Fire.

Enter this kingdom through drawbridges of tongues.
Read the braille text authored by man and weeping Gods –
that dark rain, that black page of sky; that waxed stamp of sun;
drown in fathoms of iris moats that held a million memories.

Listen to folklore of ghosts
leaving mouths as they are marooned
like mussel shells that died by rapids slowed by bone.
Look at the water, it is full of red demons –
once white as chrysanthemums on mile-wide graves.

Please do not leave this kingdom that the greatest minds built.
We must rebuild our learning before new cities,
and look into eyes of those who remain
to see hell is only made by the blind.

We are made from beautiful atoms

After Keiji Nakazawa

Remember, my sister,
we are made of beautiful atoms,
up there in the doll-eyed darkness,
our world is a teardrop from God,
no water is anywhere else but here –
remember, my sister, we are made from beautiful atoms.

Remember, my brother,
we both were born and wiped *unclean*;
that blood of birth could connect us –
our mothers are portals to beautiful atoms.
Hold on to me, brother, I shall carry you.
Remember our world was once a beautiful eye

but
none of us
saw it.

THE HUMAN BLITZ

"Germany never bombed Coventry, it was Hitler. It is always someone in power that ruins the lives of the vulnerable. I was sent away for two years as a child to live with strangers because our house was bombed. What did we children do to deserve that? I came home to one new brother and one less sister but you just have to get on with it, I suppose."

Coventry Evacuee

I passed by a woman who gave me the blitz

"My Dad worked in the mines and at the end of his life he told us that some of the bodies they pulled from the rubble looked like coal covered in crisp white cotton."
Blitz Survivor

In winter
she returns to the blitz
through bonfires of breath
and thinks of letterboxes breathing their last,
those handwritten leaves curled to orange flowers.

In winter
she is five years old again,
watching thread veins write letters
to a Dad who never spoke of what he found
at number twenty-six when he cradled slate from a crib.

In winter
she sits alone on her ottoman,
spraying her husband through Istanbul musk
and raising a glass of sherry to how he looked at twenty
before the gnaw of a nurse's pumice ate the sensual woman.

In winter
her grandchild drowned in an *Apple*
and, when she surfaced, they walked to St Michael's
to make a cathedral with both of their fingers joined.
In winter she lost her hands in the fire looking for her gollywog.

In spring
she left instructions to be cremated
and, when she danced in that new grey dress,

her granddaughter read a poem from her *Apple;*
the orange flowers curled open like fragranced letters.

Apple = iPhone

Coventry homes of Tudor wood

For Katsumi

The last survivors told yawning grandchildren
how fingers poked through rooftops as godless spires
pointing to Gods who left them with the eighth day.

Tudor houses will not survive firestorms –
sand, clay and dung rest on tar-coated wood;
imagine the smell if you add flames and collateral damage.

Picture other mosaics you never saw that burned –
a wife who worshipped her war-mute husband;
he stirred his tea for an hour watching sailors drown.

Picture the face-down deaths of firemen –
serpentine hoses thrashing unmanned water;
the rainbows they made in pools of fading eyes.

These were our flint of kin, weaving flesh through flame,
knitting their hated accents into feared machinery.
We are different cogs; our words are revolutions.

Evacuee

"Those who fight refugees from coming into their country forget that not so long ago their ancestors were refugees of war. We were called evacuees; it means the same thing."
Coventry Evacuee

The new talk was exodus,
children sent *from* Coventry,
clasping umbilical gas masks tighter than their mothers.

The manic banshee of sirens
caused Jack to wet himself;
in full-moon sky, the whites of his eyes are searchlights.

Tonight, the trains shall wail
with children playing brave;
there is no love rationed when a child is cleaved from their kin.

Postman in the smoke

For Margaret & Vic

In the smouldering amnion of new Coventry,
a singed dog dragged to water on its arse
licks the old nails deeper into its spleen.

A postman stands in the flame-grey postcode,
staring at doorways with chimneys around them,
moaning as they open to charred occupants.

The King is stuttering from the news –
a different stutter almost Germanic,
and Churchill will orate through smoke:
Dresden,
Hamburg,
Empire,
Martha's house.

Inferno

After "Wunde" by August Stramm

In Dresden
it would be a crime not to touch
wicks of fingers pointing to God,
and take gold rings engraved with their names.

Identify them.
These dead firemen's buckets filled
with initialled rings weigh heavy.

In safe rooms
flames are planned by warmongers;
the rousing speech on still tables fat with ham.

Identify them.
These men who pin faceless kings to ghosts
and tell them they did what needed to be done.

In Dresden
it is a crime to not observe silence,
to not marry yourself to the past,
to be sorry for what happened here
and there
and there
and there
and.

Koventrieren

(A word introduced after the Coventry Blitz into the German language meaning 'to completely destroy a city from the air'.)

I heard unspoken communions made
which old people keep until death beds.
The wine of your wounds on bomb-glow breasts
exposed by *Luftwaffe* and a deep-rooted shame
you had to admit before guilt and cancer ate you.

If only you had laid him three yards to the left,
you would both be arm in arm down *High Street* now.
Mother and son in a beautiful chain of events
that began in the blitz and ended in your crib.
This never happened because you fed him on time.

The art of war (II)

In Basra
they close her eyes and wash him.
The son drips silk, spins birth mist,
painting her masterpiece on sackcloth.

From mountains
a canvas of man-made stars,
apache mauve, Kalashnikov pink
the dark matter, drones.

On tarmac
a war stork births unwanted sons
swaddled in stars of folded nylon
carried from womb to wood.

At the wake
tumblers drink the men;
their eyes remove lichen,
epitaphs of watercolours.

A park near Chernobyl

After Mario Petrucci

"Silence is the only thing produced here now."
Anon

Sons hung in lockets blinking from trees.
Pounding in the stricken heart,
a father sieved dust for his daughters.

Tannoys collapsed the legs of mothers
echoing names of rush-buried men,
their blue bodies still as the moon's pale sea.

Outside, the fairground grew sick.
A cello exchanged Mozart for bread,
snails mocked the moored dodgems.

Stiff men stapled names of the dead.
Mothers flung God to ground,
retrieving photographs of sellotaped sons.

Picture the unused ferris wheel –
caged within its silence,
spent with sun's rusted rouble.

The cats that cleaned themselves
died en route to privacy;
they purred through sonar blips.

In veiled maternity wards
babes bloomed flower-heads –
their tongues were anthers.

They swept the birds up years ago,
then burnt the brooms that dared whisper
to muted streets.

Sky for a silent boy

"Let your plans be dark and impenetrable as night, and when you move,
fall like a thunderbolt."
Sun Tzu, The Art of War

And they knew one green apple could poison the others,
how western eyes would gawp from Sangin's sky;
their brothers' eyes would judge them from mountains.

And they knew when songbirds broke beaks upon the water
that all the virgins would be ruined in a village,
so they shot them for food and sang of their nests.

And they knew from the map of a hen's bloodied throat
that all the eggs would be covered in dust,
so they left them on rocks for concaved dogs.

And when the drones came, flowers closed their mouths,
a throbbing blister sutured the day's remains.
War bled sky for a silent boy.

Collateral damage

For Reuben

I heard of a doorway tied to wooden pegs
and women entered to bathe the grandmother with milk.
The pregnant offered their breasts to bowls –
all of them wore black in the midday sun.
Men gathered any wood they could find,
laid her to rest on walking sticks, fruit crates –
and driftwood of a cot that sailed away from its occupant.

I heard of a canvas mansion stretching eight miles long,
visible from the flickering chandeliers of earth;
heaven blown out as lights leave billowing eyes.
In this home, a doctor is dragging pans to the well,
picking out flies and remnants of parched mouths
who beat him to it by chance of where they live.
His cracked heels are blueprints of displacement;
he is watching his mother go home from the flames.

Before the new bombs fall

When evening came,
a mother made a wish as her newborn suckled.
The milk's slow timbre a beautiful drone,
she fed him one last time in the crosshairs.

When evening came,
mother and son exploded like pomegranate trees,
and birdsong resumed again just like the Somme,
trenches plump with children.

When evening ends for children and butterflies,
they unroll their tongues like scrolls for the dead
writing their names across a village of sky –
the gluttonous Gods are never full.

The Gods

For Samantha

Today we killed God with our lips.
I wrapped a boy in the lying flag,
hair soft as Buddhist chants;
his mother swore at a soot-heavy sky.

The day we wept in the bloodstained bazaar,
you traded tenderness in the bullet-ridden silks
and wrung linen sent from England into the gutter –
a mother's mouth screamed with no sound coming out.

Today we were busy being fastened from liquor.
A man threw a bag, screaming God's many names,
and took a boy, and a son, and father and kin.
All of the streets came alive in their deaths.

How to survive a nuclear winter

"The unleashed power of the atom has changed everything save our modes of thinking and we thus drift toward unparalleled catastrophe."
Albert Einstein

Beneath the welt of a nuclear moon,
we'll meet in government shelters,
sing merry cockney songs in subways foggy with stench;
help will come in books of flames.

All the cars are gunmetal grey;
we harvest screen-wash for wounds.
At night, marauders make smog from bodies in acres of lye –
they wheel the meat to the ice rink.

We catch crows to feed them turnips; if they live, we eat them.
At night, we collect hair from Kylie's comb;
it stops her child from bawling.

In meagre hours of daylight,
we smash mirrors to keep us pretty.
Kylie went mad there, took her own life
by shouting rebel poems to child lieutenants.

We do not go by days but by schedules, and they can kill you.
Last week we saw sun for the first time in weeks;
they shot six people roaming in wonderment.

The next time moon burns through ragged fallout,
I'll loiter on the rubble of my house,
yelling war poems by Edith Sitwell,
waiting for haggard children –
the jurors of russet knives.

Dots that never become full stops

....
....
....
....
....
....
....
....
....
....
....
....
....
....
....
....
....
....
....
....
....
....
....
....
....

Data:

1. The black dots represent nuclear tests conducted since the bombing of Hiroshima and Nagasaki in 1945. The total number: 2058.

2. The majority of tests were conducted between 1945-1998 by America and USSR.

3. You would need approximately another seven pages of these black dots to represent the number of nuclear weapons in the world today.

Sources for 1. and 2. include CTBTO (Preparatory commission for the comprehensive nuclear-test-ban treaty organisation) and Nuclear time lapse map by Isao Hashimoto.
Source 3: Ploughshares Fund (March 2016) reported the recent estimated nuclear stockpiles are 15,375.

Other statistics indicate there are under 5,000 large cities in the world.

Acknowledgements

Acknowledgements and thanks are due to the editors of the following magazines and publications where these poems and translations first appeared:

Magma, Morning Star, Coal Sack Magazine (Japan)*, *Poetry International* (Europe)*, *International Times, The Bogman's Cannon* (EIRE), *The Poets Republic, Poems for Jeremy Corbyn* (Shoestring Press), *Ink Sweat & Tears, I am not a silent poet, O-Dark Thirty Review, The Beacon, Proletarian Poetry,* Shabda Press anthology *Nuclear Impact: Broken Atoms in Our Hands* (USA), *Deep Water Literary Journal* (EIRE), *The Rising Phoenix Review* (USA), *Maverick,* Pighog Press, *Here Comes Everyone, Eunoia Review, The Curly Mind, Fireplaces, Greystone, Two Nineteen, Kauro* (China)*, *Peaceful Schools* (UK), *denotes translated works.

'Fat Man' was one of a few poems selected by Poetry International (Europe) from European poets and essayists for translation in their 2015 anthology for bombed cities which was titled *Steden Schuilen Niet (Cities Do Not Hide).*

'How to Make a Japanese Flag' was nominated by *Deep Water Literary Journal* in 2015 as one of their *"Best of the Net"* poems.

'Pearl Harbour' was voted by the public as the winner of the September 2015 "poem of the month" competition at *Ink Sweat & Tears.*

'The Art of War (I)' features on Peaceful Schools UK website where Antony Owen is listed as a "Poet for Peace".

The sequence of Senryu / Haiku was featured in *Kauro Journal* (China) and also featured at The Chapel of Unity (Coventry Cathedral) and The Peace Centre (Hiroshima ICC).

Senryu (I) is planned to be featured in Truman on Trial which is in a national educational resource for schools by CND Peace Education UK. Many have been taught at monthly poetry workshops in Hiroshima, hosted by Prof R. Klein (Jogakuin University), and others taught in peace education schools held at Jogakuin (Hiroshima), Cardinal Newman School (Coventry), Positive Images Festival and Coventry Peace Festival. Some of these poems have also been aired on Brum Radio, Hillz FM and BBC CWR.

The author wishes to convey his dearest thanks to John Hartley and Hideko Okamoto of the Coventry Hiroshima club for arranging his extensive trip to Hiroshima in May 2015. He would also like to thank the courage of both atomic bomb survivors, Sueko and Keiko, for sharing their testimonies with him.

The author also wants to acknowledge his appreciation to Sarah and Ruth at V. Press for their incredible support and enthusiasm throughout the whole editorial process.

V.

Antony Owen was born in 1973, Coventry, and raised by working class parents. *The Nagasaki Elder* is his fifth collection of poetry, jointly inspired by growing up in Cold War Britain at the peak of nuclear proliferation and, more recently, a self-funded trip to Hiroshima in 2015 to hear testimonies of Atomic bomb survivors.

Owen's war poetry and haiku have been translated into Japanese, Mandarin and Dutch in anthologies and journals including *Poetry International* (Europe) and *Coal Sack Publications* (Japan).

In recognition of his 2015 peace trip to Hiroshima, CND Peace Education (UK) selected Owen as one of their first national patrons, and he won a Peace & Reconciliation award in 2016 for Community Cohesion from his home city of Coventry. A trip to Dresden and Nagasaki is planned for 2019 to continue his dedication to contemporary war poetry and transmitting art with a social conscience.

Owen's work, which ranges across the polemic, political and personal, has received widespread acclaim by critics and his contemporaries. Previous reviews have featured in *Morning Star, Southword, Sabotage* and *Stride*.

Previous collections

Margaret Thatcher's Museum (2015, Hesterglock Press)
The Year I Loved England (2014, Pighog Press) Joseph Horgan & Antony Owen
The Dreaded Boy (2011, Pighog Press,)
My Father's Eyes Were Blue (2009, Heaventree Press)

V.